Natural Disasters

Tsunamis

by
Samantha Bonar

Consultant:
Dr. Walter C. Dudley
Professor of Oceanography
University of Hawaii at Hilo

Chair, Scientific Advisory Council
Pacific Tsunami Museum

CAPSTONE
HIGH-INTEREST
BOOKS

an imprint of Capstone Press
Mankato, Minnesota

Capstone High-Interest Books are published by Capstone Press
151 Good Counsel Drive, P.O. Box 669, Mankato, Minnesota 56002
http://www.capstone-press.com

Library of Congress Cataloging-in-Publication Data
Bonar, Samantha.
    Tsunamis/by Samantha Bonar.
    p. cm.—(Natural disasters)
    Includes bibliographical references and index.
    ISBN 0-7368-0902-3
    1. Tsunamis—Juvenile literature. [1. Tsunamis.] I. Title. II. Series.
GC221.5 .B66 2002
363.34'9—dc21   00-012818

Summary: Explains why tsunamis occur, the damage they inflict, some famous
tsunamis, and how people can protect themselves against these giant waves.

Editorial Credits
Tom Adamson, editor; Lois Wallentine, product planning editor; Timothy Halldin,
    cover designer and illustrator; Katy Kudela, photo researcher

Photo Credits
Courtesy of NOAA's Pacific Marine Environmental Laboratory, 22, 26
NOAA, 4, 7, 8, 10, 24, 30, 34, 36
The Pacific Tsunami Museum, 14, 16 (all), 20, 29, 32, 38, 40, 42
Rick Doyle/The Viesti Collection, Inc., cover

1 2 3 4 5 6 07 06 05 04 03 02

Table of Contents

Chapter 1

Tsunamis

The summer sun was setting in Papua New Guinea when villagers heard a loud boom. The earth began to shake. People saw the ocean slowly withdraw from the shore. Curious people gathered at the beach because they could see the exposed ocean floor.

The villagers then heard a roar. The roar sounded like a jet plane approaching. A wall of water appeared. The large wave moved quickly toward the beach. People ran away. But it was too late. The wave knocked them down.

Another larger wave swept in. It reached all the way to the villages. It smashed houses and threw people into trees. A third wave hit. The waves were as high as 40 feet (12 meters).

Tsunami waves flattened houses that stood on this beach in Papua New Guinea.

They rushed more than 1,600 feet (500 meters) inland.

Ita Atopi was carrying her 1-month-old twins in slings attached to her body. She let the waves carry her and the babies. She grabbed a floating coconut tree and held on. Atopi and the twins survived.

More than 2,200 people died. Many more people were hurt. Pieces of houses hung from the tops of palm trees.

This disaster happened on July 17, 1998, in Papua New Guinea. It was one of the worst tsunamis in history. The disaster began with an earthquake. This sudden violent shaking of the ground caused a large underwater landslide. In turn, the landslide caused the tsunami.

Tsunamis

A tsunami (soo-NAH-mee) is a huge wave or series of waves. Tsunami is a Japanese word. "Tsu" means "harbor." "Nami" means "wave." Tsunami waves can be as high as 100 feet

Tsunami waves carried this school building 213 feet (65 meters).

(30 meters) when they reach shore. This height is as tall as a 10-story building.

A tsunami can occur in any ocean. But most tsunamis occur in the Pacific Ocean. Earthquakes that happen on the ocean floor are the most common cause of tsunamis. Underwater landslides and volcanoes also can

Several hundred houses once stood on this stretch of land in Papua New Guinea.

cause tsunamis. Volcanoes are mountains that sometimes erupt with lava, hot gases, and ash.

Tsunamis can travel across the entire ocean. In 1960, an earthquake off the coast of Chile caused a tsunami. This tsunami traveled 10,500 miles (17,000 kilometers) to Japan. The tsunami killed more than 100 Japanese people.

Tsunamis can occur with little warning. They can destroy entire coastal towns. People sometimes have only a few minutes to move to higher ground.

Tsunamis are uncommon. But they can occur any time of the day or night. They can happen year-round. Scientists are working on better ways to predict tsunamis. Warning systems can help save lives.

Chapter 2

Why Tsunamis Happen

People sometimes call tsunamis tidal waves. But this is incorrect. Tsunamis are not caused by tides. Tides are the rising and falling of the ocean's surface. These changes in the ocean's level are caused by the pull of the moon and the sun. This pull is called gravity. Tides usually happen twice each day.

Tsunamis are caused by sudden movements of the ocean floor. Underwater earthquakes, landslides, or volcanic eruptions can cause these movements. A large meteorite falling from space or an above-water landslide also could cause a tsunami.

A tsunami can scatter debris over a wide area.

Stages of a Tsunami

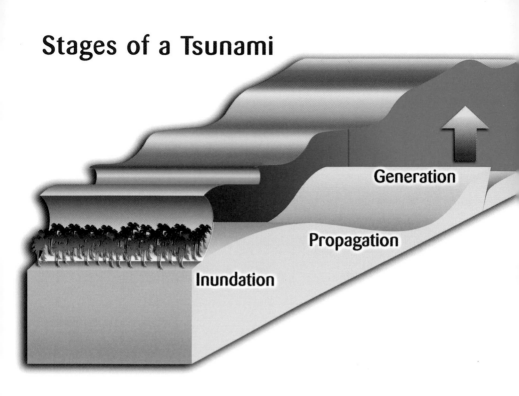

Generation

Propagation

Inundation

Waves

Most ocean waves are caused by wind. These waves move on the surface of the water. But tsunami waves extend from the surface to the bottom of the ocean.

Waves are measured by their period and wavelength. The period is the time it takes two wave crests to pass the same point. A wave's crest is the highest part of the wave. The wavelength is the distance between two wave crests. Waves caused by wind have a period of 5 to 20 seconds. Their wavelength is usually about 100 feet (30 meters). A tsunami's period can range from 10 minutes to two hours. Its wavelength can be as long as 100 miles (160 kilometers).

How a Tsunami Starts

A tsunami goes through three stages. The first stage is generation. Generation is the process that creates a tsunami.

An underwater earthquake, landslide, or volcanic eruption makes the ocean floor move. The ocean floor either lifts or drops. It can move several feet or meters. This shift forces up a large section of water. The water then moves away from the point of the shift in all directions. The same thing happens when a rock is thrown into a pond. A circle of ripples moves away from where the rock entered the water.

Waves rush inland during the inundation stage.

Tsunami Speed

The second stage of a tsunami is called propagation. During this stage, the tsunami moves away from its source.

Tsunami waves move quickly in deep ocean water. The deeper the water, the faster they travel. Tsunami waves can move faster than 600 miles (970 kilometers) per hour. That is as fast as a jet airplane. Tsunami waves can move from one side of the Pacific Ocean to the other in less than one day.

In the deep ocean, a tsunami does not form a high wave. It might be only a few feet or meters high. It could pass under ships. The people on the ships would not notice the tsunami.

The tsunami waves slow down as they move to shallower water near land. At the same time, the waves become taller. They may reach a height of 100 feet (30 meters).

Flooding

The third stage of a tsunami is called inundation. The tsunami waves move onto and flood dry land.

A tsunami may behave in different ways when it reaches shore. Some coastlines are steep. The tsunami waves may only travel a few feet or meters inland at these coasts. Other areas have gradually sloping coastlines.

Inundation

This tsunami struck Hawaii in 1946. A powerful earthquake near Alaska created the tsunami.

The tsunami arrived as a quickly rising tide.

Turbulent water flooded inland. Strong currents carried debris back into the ocean.

The water can move further inland on these coasts. For example, Papua New Guinea's coast slopes gradually. The tsunami's water there reached as far as 10,000 feet (3,000 meters) inland in some areas.

A tsunami may behave in different ways as it reaches shore. It may arrive as a quickly rising tide that floods inland. The tsunami also may arrive as a series of towering waves. These waves may break on the shore. A wave breaks when it collapses downward.

The most destructive type of wave is called a bore. This steep wall of water moves very quickly. A bore can be as tall as 100 feet (30 meters).

The same tsunami may affect coastal areas differently. In some places, it may cause major damage. As it rushes inland, it may uproot trees and crush houses. Trees, people, and debris can be carried along with the water. Debris can include wood from destroyed buildings, pieces of ships, or anything else in

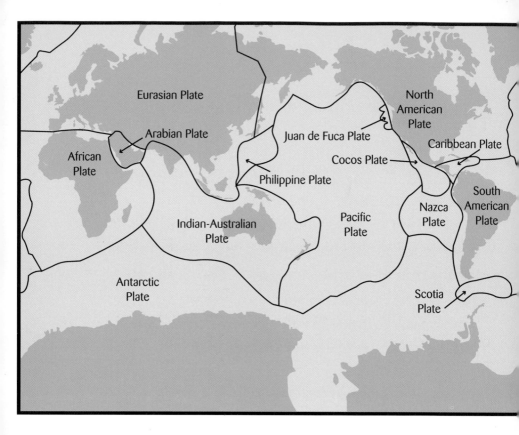

the tsunami's path. Tsunamis can move large boulders that weigh several tons. In other areas, there may only be minor flooding.

The tsunami withdraws when it has run as far inland as it can go. It sucks people and loose objects back into the ocean.

The Ring of Fire

Most tsunamis occur in the Pacific Ocean. The Pacific is the world's largest ocean. It covers more than one-third of Earth's surface. It is surrounded by a ring of mountain chains, deep ocean trenches, and islands. Many volcanoes and earthquakes occur in this area. This area is called the "ring of fire."

Earth's outer layer is called the crust. The crust is made up of large moving plates made of rock. The crust consists of about 10 large plates and several smaller plates. They move very slowly. These continental plates also cover the bottom of the oceans. Most earthquakes occur where the plates meet. Many of the plates meet in the ring of fire.

Large earthquakes have occurred in areas off the coasts of Alaska, Russia, and South America. These earthquakes caused tsunamis that traveled all the way across the Pacific.

Tsunamis can wash away bridges.

The Cascadia Subduction Zone
The Cascadia Subduction Zone is an area off the coast of Oregon and Washington. The Juan de Fuca plate and the North American plate meet in this area. The Juan de Fuca plate is forcing its way underneath the North American plate.

New evidence suggests that a major earthquake may occur in the Cascadia Subduction Zone every 300 to 500 years. The last major earthquake there may have been in 1700. Scientists think this earthquake triggered a tsunami. The tsunami waves may have crashed on shore at the Washington or Oregon coasts. Ocean sand has been found in forests in this area. The sand probably was carried there by the tsunami.

Chapter 3

Warning Systems

Scientists cannot predict when an earthquake or a tsunami will occur. But they know a tsunami may form after an earthquake occurs offshore.

Predicting Tsunamis

A large earthquake may cause a Pacific-wide tsunami. This type of tsunami travels all the way across the Pacific Ocean. An underwater earthquake or landslide near a coastline may cause a local tsunami. This type of tsunami only affects the nearby coastline.

By studying past tsunamis, scientists may be able to predict the size of a tsunami. The

This buoy will help determine if a dangerous tsunami has occurred. ◁

In 1992, tsunami waves washed away all plants and trees from this area in Indonesia.

shape of a coastline or harbor also affects the impact of a tsunami. For example, tall coastal cliffs can help block a tsunami. Scientists can look at maps of coastlines to find out where the most damage might occur.

Tsunami Warning Systems

Scientists have established warning systems to save lives. The United States has two main tsunami warning centers. These centers are in Alaska and Hawaii.

The Tsunami Warning System (TWS) is made up of 26 member countries that border the Pacific Ocean. The member countries include the United States, Canada, Chile, Japan, and Russia. These countries study earthquakes and issue warnings if they think a tsunami might threaten a coast.

The Pacific Tsunami Warning Center (PTWC) is part of the TWS. It is located near Honolulu, Hawaii. This center issues tsunami warnings to most of the countries that border the Pacific Ocean.

The West Coast and Alaska Tsunami Warning Center is in Palmer, Alaska. It was established after a deadly tsunami struck Alaska and California in 1964. This center issues warnings about tsunamis to the Canadian and U.S. western coasts.

The National Tsunami Hazard Mitigation Program

The U.S. government set up the National Tsunami Hazard Mitigation Program (NTHMP) in 1997. This program works to improve tsunami warning systems.

The NTHMP is building ocean buoys that can measure tsunamis as they pass. These buoys are called Deep-ocean Assessment and Reporting of Tsunamis (DART) buoys. The DART buoys are as big as cars. They float on the surface of the ocean. They are connected to pressure recorders on the ocean floor. A tsunami will push more water on top of the recorder. The recorder will detect this pressure. The pressure recorders then will send this information to the buoys. Satellites or radios then will send the information to warning centers.

Scientists believe the buoys will help make tsunami warnings more accurate. Scientists will be able to detect a tsunami while it is still in the deep part of the ocean.

Scientists believe that the DART buoys will make tsunami warnings more accurate.

Six of these detection stations soon will be located throughout the Pacific Ocean. Three buoys will be located off the coast of Alaska. Two others will be placed off the western coast of North America. The sixth one will go off the western coast of South America.

Other Warning Systems

The NTHMP uses computers to create inundation maps of coastlines in California, Oregon, Washington, Alaska, and Hawaii. These maps help scientists figure out where flooding would be the worst. The maps also help scientists plan evacuation routes. These routes help people move away from dangerous areas.

The Pacific Marine Environmental Laboratory set up a global tsunami e-mail network. The network helps tsunami researchers around the world communicate quickly when a tsunami occurs.

Scientists want to develop better warning systems. About 75 percent of tsunami

Tsunamis can cause great damage to buildings.

warnings issued since the 1950s have been
false alarms. False alarms are expensive. In
1986, Honolulu was evacuated after a warning
that later proved to be a false alarm. This
evacuation cost $30 million in lost salaries
and business activity.

Chapter 4

The Power of a Tsunami

Tsunamis are a threat to anyone living near an ocean. In the 1990s, tsunamis killed more than 5,000 people worldwide. Destructive tsunamis occur in the Pacific Ocean about once each year. Pacific-wide tsunamis only happen about once every 10 years.

The Papua New Guinea tsunami of 1998 was one of the worst tsunamis of the last 100 years. But many other tsunamis have caused great damage and loss of life.

Tsunamis around the World

More than one-quarter of all tsunamis since 1895 occurred near Japan. The country has

In 1993, a tsunami that occurred in Japan flattened buildings and killed more than 120 people.

The 1946 tsunami picked up and moved houses in Hawaii.

been hit by about 150 tsunamis in the last century. Japan is located near the point where four continental plates meet. Japanese people have planted shoreline forests and built seawalls to help block tsunami waves.

Most tsunamis in the United States have hit Alaska and Hawaii. Tsunamis also have occurred along the coasts of Central and South America. A tsunami that hit Nicaragua in 1992 killed 116 people. Tsunamis also have hit Indonesia and islands in the Pacific Ocean.

East Indies, 1883

The worst tsunami in recorded history occurred in the East Indies on August 27, 1883. A volcanic island called Krakatoa near Indonesia erupted. Before the eruption, this island was 2,667 feet (813 meters) above sea level. The huge eruption completely destroyed the island.

The volcano collapsed into the ocean. The underwater explosion caused a tsunami that was about 130 feet (40 meters) high. It killed more than 30,000 people and destroyed 165 villages on the surrounding islands.

Aleutian Islands, 1946

On April 1, 1946, an earthquake in the Aleutian Islands near Alaska produced a powerful tsunami. The tsunami reached Unimak Island in less than one hour. A wave 100 feet (30 meters) high destroyed

A powerful tsunami caused a great deal of damage in Hilo, Hawaii, in 1960.

a five-story lighthouse on the island. All five people inside the lighthouse were killed.

The tsunami crossed the Pacific Ocean as fast as a jet plane. It reached Hawaii in less than five hours. Even after crossing the ocean, it still had the power to create waves 50 feet (15 meters) high. In all, the tsunami killed 165 people. The Pacific Tsunami Warning Center opened in Hawaii after this tsunami.

Chile, 1960

On May 22, 1960, a large earthquake occurred off Chile's coast. About 200 people got into boats and went to sea to escape the shaking. The tsunami hit the coast about 15 minutes after the earthquake. All of these people were killed.

The tsunami moved across the ocean and killed 61 people in Hawaii. In Hilo, Hawaii, the force of the tsunami bent parking meters flat on their sides. The tsunami also came ashore in Crescent City, California, about 15 hours after the earthquake. It caused minor damage and flooding there. Together, the tsunami and the earthquake caused as many as 2,000 deaths.

Alaska, 1964

On March 28, 1964, a major earthquake hit Prince William Sound, Alaska. Almost 77,000 square miles (200,000 square kilometers) of the ocean floor moved. This movement caused a series of tsunami waves. Within three minutes, waves completely destroyed the Valdez, Alaska, waterfront.

At nearby Seward, Alaska, the earthquake destroyed several fuel tanks. A 33-foot (10-meter) tsunami wave was covered with burning oil from the tanks. The wave appeared to be on fire. More waves spread the fire onshore.

The earthquake created tsunamis as far away as California and Oregon. At least 122 people died. The West Coast and Alaska Tsunami Warning Center opened as a result of this tsunami. This center is in Palmer, Alaska.

The 1964 Alaska tsunami shoved a wooden plank through a truck tire in Whittier, Alaska.

Chapter 5

Surviving a Tsunami

Tsunami warning centers can detect earthquakes that are likely to produce tsunamis. They can give an approximate time the tsunami might reach a certain place. But they cannot tell how big the tsunami waves will be. They cannot be certain where the tsunami will cause the most damage.

Feeling an Earthquake

Tsunamis sometimes begin close to shore. There is no time for an official warning for these tsunamis. People who live along the coast should immediately move inland during an earthquake. They should not wait for an official warning.

Tsunami waves can move thousands of feet or meters inland.

A tsunami wave can move much faster than a person can run.

An earthquake may happen far enough away that it cannot be felt. But it may still generate a tsunami that can travel a long way. The Pacific and Alaska Tsunami Warning Centers will issue warnings to threatened communities. A warning can give people enough time to move inland.

In 1993, an earthquake hit the coast of Okushiri, Japan. People left their homes and rushed inland. This tsunami killed 200 people. But many more people would have died if they had not evacuated.

Warning Signs
People who live near coasts should know a tsunami's warning signs. People may see the ocean suddenly withdraw from the shore. People also may hear a loud roar. These people should quickly move inland. People should never wait to see the wave. People who can see the wave are too close to escape. A tsunami wave can move much faster than a person can run.

Tsunamis usually are made up of many waves. The first wave might not be the largest. The waves can keep coming for up to eight hours. People should not return home until an official notice tells them it is safe. People should stay tuned to their local radio and TV stations during a tsunami emergency. They will

Tsunamis sometimes arrive as a wall of water.

hear warnings and announcements that will tell them what they should do.

Tsunamis can travel up rivers and streams that are connected to the ocean. People should stay away from rivers and streams during a tsunami warning.

People sometimes do not have time to move to higher ground. These people should go to the closest high-rise building that is made of reinforced concrete. The top floor of such a building can be a safe place. People should not stay in homes and small buildings near the coast. These types of buildings usually cannot withstand a tsunami.

People cannot stop tsunamis. But people who know their warning signs and obey safety instructions can survive them.

Words to Know

debris (duh-BREE)—the remains of something that has been destroyed

earthquake (URTH-kwayk)—a sudden, violent shaking of the ground; a shifting of Earth's crust causes this shaking.

evacuate (i-VAK-yoo-ate)—to move away from an area because of danger

generation (jen-uh-RAY-shuhn)—the creation of a tsunami

inland (IN-luhnd)—away from the ocean

inundation (in-uhn-DAY-shuhn)—flooding on dry land caused by a tsunami

landslide (LAND-slide)—a sudden slide of earth and rocks down a hill or mountain

propagation (praw-puh-GAY-shuhn)—the movement of a tsunami away from its source

volcano (vol-KAY-noh)—a mountain with vents through which hot gases, ash, and lava sometimes erupt

To Learn More ⟵

Drohan, Michele Ingber. *Tsunamis: Killer Waves*. Natural Disasters. New York: PowerKids Press, 1999.

Lassieur, Allison. *Earthquakes*. Natural Disasters. Mankato, Minn.: Capstonc High-Interest Books, 2001.

Lassieur, Allison. *Volcanoes*. Natural Disasters. Mankato, Minn.: Capstone High-Interest Books, 2001.

Meister, Cari. *Earthquakes*. Nature's Fury. Minneapolis: Abdo, 1999.

Thompson, Luke. *Tsunamis*. Natural Disasters. New York: Children's Press, 2000.

⟶ Useful Addresses

Pacific Marine Environmental Laboratory
7600 Sand Point Way NE
Seattle, WA 98115-6349

Pacific Tsunami Museum
P.O. Box 806
Hilo, HI 96721

Pacific Tsunami Warning Center
91-270 Fort Weaver Road
Ewa Beach, HI 96706

**West Coast and Alaska Tsunami Warning
  Center**
910 South Felton Street
Palmer, AK 99645

Internet Sites

**Federal Emergency Management Agency—
Tsunami**
http://www.fema.gov/library/tsunami.htm

**The National Tsunami Hazard Mitigation
Program**
http://www.pmel.noaa.gov/tsunami-hazard

Pacific Disaster Center
http://www.pdc.org/pdc/pub/frmain06.htm

Pacific Tsunami Museum
http://www.tsunami.org

Tsunami!
http://www.geophys.washington.edu/tsunami

Tsunamis and Earthquakes
http://walrus.wr.usgs.gov/tsunami

Index